Student Support Materials for

AQA

A2 BIOLOGY
SPECIFICATION (B)

Module 5: Environment

Mike Boyle
Series editor: Mike Bailey

This booklet has been designed to support the AQA Biology A2 specification. It contains some material which has been added in order to clarify the specification. The examination will be limited to material set out in the specification document.

Published by HarperCollins*Publishers* Limited
77–85 Fulham Palace Road
Hammersmith
London
W6 8JB

www.**Collins**Education.com
Online support for schools and colleges

© HarperCollins*Publishers* Limited 2001
First published 2001, Reprinted 2002

ISBN 0 00 7124171

Mike Boyle asserts the moral right to be identified as the author of this work.

British Library Cataloguing in Publication Data
A catalogue record for this publication is available from the British Library

Editor: Kathryn Senior
Front cover designed by Chi Leung
Design by Barking Dog Art, Gloucestershire
Printed and bound by Scotprint, Haddington

The publisher wishes to thank the Assessment and Qualifications Alliance for permission to reproduce the examination questions.

You might also like to visit
www.**fire**and**water**.com
The book lover's website

Other useful texts

Full colour textbooks
Collins Advanced Modular Sciences: Biology AS, Biology A2 and *A2 Option Applied Ecology*
Collins Advanced Science: Biology and *Human Biology*

Student Support Booklets
AQA (B) Biology: 1 Core Principles
AQA (B) Biology: 2 Genes and Genetic Engineering
AQA (B) Biology: 3 Physiology and Transport
AQA (B) Biology: 4 Energy, Continuity and Control

What books do I need to study this course?

You will probably use a range of resources during your course. Some will be produced by the centre where you are studying, some by a commercial publisher and others may be borrowed from libraries or study centres. Different resources have different uses – but remember, owning a book is not enough – it must be *used*.

What does this booklet cover?

This *Student Support Booklet* covers the content you need to know and understand to pass the module test for AQA Biology A2 *Module 5: Environment*. It is very concise and you will need to study it carefully to make sure you can remember all of the material.

How can I remember all this material?

Reading the booklet is an essential first step – but reading by itself is not a good way to get stuff into your memory. If you have bought the booklet and can write on it, you could try the following techniques to help you to memorise the material:

- underline or highlight the most important words in every paragraph
- underline or highlight scientific jargon – write a note of the meaning in the margin if you are unsure
- remember the number of items in a list – then you can tell if you have forgotten one when you try to remember it later
- tick sections when you are sure you know them – and then concentrate on the sections you do not yet know.

How can I check my progress?

The module test at the end is a useful check on your progress – you may want to wait until you have nearly completed the module and use it as a mock exam or try questions one by one as you progress. The answers show you how much you need to do to get the marks.

What if I get stuck?

The colour textbook *Collins Advanced Modular Sciences: Biology A2* is designed to support your A2 course. It provides more explanation than this booklet. It may help you to make progress if you get stuck.

Any other good advice?

- You will not learn well if you are tired or stressed. Set aside time for work (and play!) and try to stick to it.
- Don't leave everything until the last minute – whatever your friends may tell you it doesn't work.
- You are most effective if you work hard for shorter periods of time and then take a (short!) break. 30 minutes of work followed by a five or ten minute break is a useful pattern. Then get back to work.
- Some people work better in the morning, some in the evening. Find out which works better for you and do that whenever possible.
- Do not suffer in silence – ask friends and your teacher for help.
- Stay calm, enjoy it and … good luck!

The main text gives a very concise explanation of the ideas in your course. You must study all of it – none is spare or not needed.

The examiner's notes are always useful – make sure you read them because they will help with your module test.

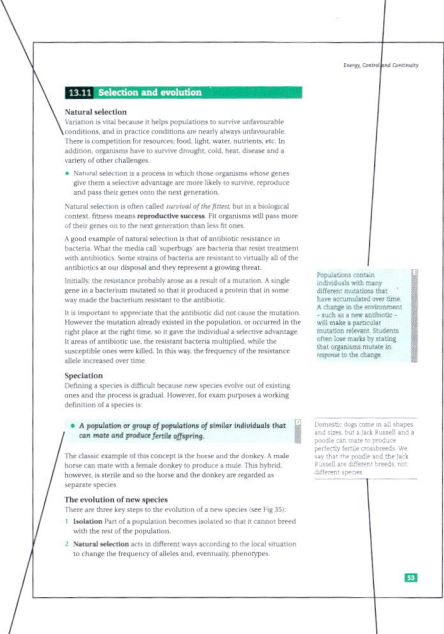

There are rigorous definitions of the main terms used in your examination – memorise these exactly.

Further explanation references give a little extra detail, or directs you to other texts if you need more help or need to read around a topic.

Unit overview and revision planner

Section	Contents	Revision complete
14.1 Energy flow through ecosystems	• Energy transfer through ecosystems • Food chains and food webs • Pyramids of numbers, biomass and energy	
14.2 Minerals are recycled in ecosystems	• The role of decomposers • The carbon cycle • The nitrogen cycle	
14.3 Studying ecosystems	• Ecological techniques; quadrats/transects • Measurement of abiotic factors • Statistics – chi squared and standard deviation	
14.4 Dynamics of ecosystems	• Ecosystems, communities, populations and niches • Population dynamics; limiting factors and carrying capacity • Development of ecosystems – colonisation, succession and climax communities	
14.5. Man's effect on the environment	• Impact of farming • Pesticide toxicity - bioaccumulation • Balance of food production and conservation	

About this module

This unit is about **ecology** – the study of organisms in their natural surroundings. When you look at the specification, you might think that this unit is much shorter than the others, but don't be mislead by the apparent lack of content. With ecology the emphasis is on principles and examples, and there is less factual information that needs to be learned. The examination will contain a good proportion of questions involving data analysis. You will be given some new information and asked to interpret it in the light of the principles you have learned in this unit. It is therefore important that you practise examination questions such as those featured at the end of the booklet.

14.1 Energy flow through ecosystems

It is important to start with some definitions - these will revise and update your GCSE ecology.

D

- **Producers** *are organisms that can photosynthesise. They produce organic compounds such as sugars from inorganic compounds such as carbon dioxide and water. Plants, algae and photosynthetic bacteria are all producers.*

- **Consumers** *are organisms that cannot make their own organic molecules, and so must obtain them ready-made from other organisms. Animals, fungi and most bacteria are consumers.*

- **Saprophytes** *are decomposers that break down dead organic matter by extracellular digestion. Mainly bacteria or fungi, they secrete enzymes and absorb the soluble products of digestion.*

- **Food chain** *– a simple diagram that shows what-eats-what in an ecosystem. The arrows show the flow of energy. Food chains are of limited use because many animals eat more the one species. The number of steps in a food chain is usually limited to 3 of 4 because the energy runs out (Fig 1a).*

- **Food web** *– a more complex diagram that attempts to show the feeding relationships within an ecosystem (Fig 1b).*

- **Trophic level** *– a 'feeding' level in the food web. The first trophic level usually consists of producers, though detritivores (see below) can also support a food web. The next trophic level is the primary consumers (usually herbivores), then secondary consumers (carnivores) and sometimes tertiary consumers or even higher (Fig 1c). Some animals are omnivorous e.g. rats, pigs and monkeys. They have a very varied diet and so can occupy more than one trophic level.*

- **Autotrophs** *make their own food using an external energy source - usually sunlight – and a simple inorganic supply of carbon (usually carbon dioxide). Photoautotrophs make their own food by photosynthesis, while chemoautotrophs (which are all bacteria) make their own food using energy from chemical reactions. All producers are autotrophs.*

- **Heterotrophs** *cannot make their own food; they must obtain food molecules ready-made from their surroundings. All consumers are heterotrophs.*

- **Detritivore** *– an animal that feeds off detritus (rotting organic matter such as dead leaves, faeces). An earthworm is an example of a detritivore. Detritivores should not be confused with saprophytes; detritivores are animals with intestines that actually eat the detritus. Saprophytes have no intestines and feed by extracellular digestion.*

- **Humus** *– rotting organic matter in soil. This is a sticky mass of dead plants, dead animals and faeces that is being broken down by saprophytes. Humus is vital to soil because it gives it texture and allows it to holds more water. Saprophytes act on humus to release the nutrients – such as nitrate – that plants need to grow.*

Fig 1

a A simple food chain

b A food web for a British woodland

c Trophic levels

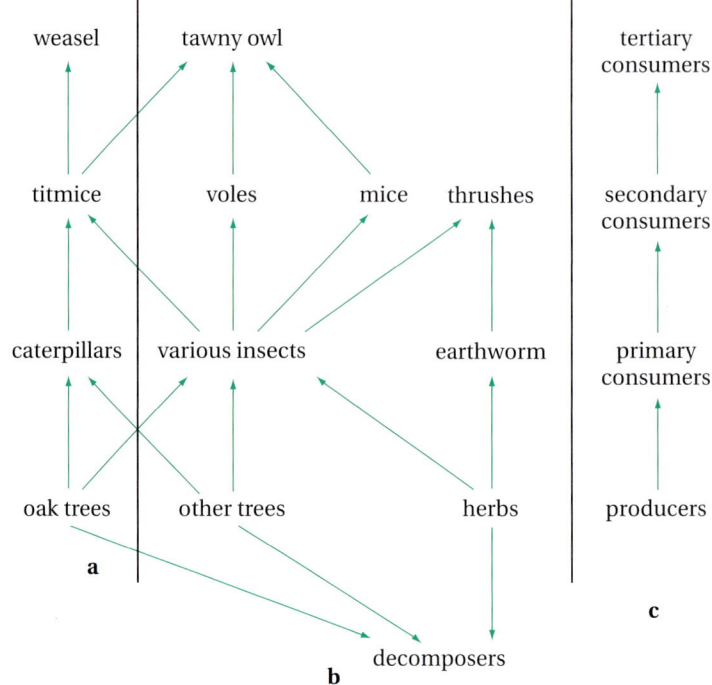

Basic principles

- The elements that form the molecules in living things – carbon, hydrogen, oxygen, nitrogen and others – are finite; i.e. there is a limited amount available.

- These elements are recycled – used again and again in different organisms.

- Recycling needs energy, mostly provided by the sun.

- Energy is not recycled – it constantly lost as heat and must be replaced.

- If the sun stopped shining, recycling would stop and so, eventually, would life on Earth (assuming the planet didn't freeze beforehand).

The importance of photosynthesis

Photosynthesis is the only process that can capture sunlight energy and so is the major route by which energy enters an ecosystem. In photosynthesis, sunlight is used to reduce carbon dioxide into organic molecules. Initially, simple carbohydrates (sugars) are made, but plants can make the other molecules such as lipids, proteins and nucleic acids by modifying the carbohydrates. In this way, plants make the food molecules that support whole ecosystems. The by-product of photosynthesis is oxygen – another substance vital to life on earth. Organisms that can photosynthesise are called producers. The relationship between producers and other types of organism in the ecosystem are shown in Table 1.

E Make sure that you are clear about organic and inorganic molecules. Organic molecules contain carbon backbones.

Put simply, photosynthesis captures energy; respiration releases it.

Type of organism	What they need	What they produce
Producers (green plants)	Carbon dioxide, inorganic ions	Oxygen, organic molecules
Consumers (mainly animals)	Organic molecules, oxygen	Carbon dioxide, organic waste
Decomposers (bacteria / fungi)	Organic molecules, oxygen	Carbon dioxide, inorganic ions (nitrate etc)*

Table 1
The relationship between producers, decomposers and consumers

* Only bacteria produce inorganic ions

Energy transfer in ecosystems

A huge amount of solar energy reaches our planet but only a small percentage is captured by plants in photosynthesis and packaged into organic molecules. The rest is lost…

- A large amount misses plants altogether; some of it heats up the atmosphere; some of heats up the seas and rocks.

- Not all the light that reaches the plant hits the chloroplasts – some passes straight through.

- Some light is of the wrong wavelength – plants use mainly the blue and red light in the visible spectrum, reflecting green. Some energy us used up in the evaporation of water from the leaves (transpiration).

- The reactions of photosynthesis, like all reactions, are inefficient – some energy is always lost as heat.

- The term **gross primary production** refers to the total energy in the organic molecules produced by a plant. However, the plant uses a proportion of the energy for it's own needs – this energy is released when the plant respires or dies and decomposes. Only the surplus produced by the plant – the **net primary production** – is available to the rest of the ecosystem.

Fig 2 shows the energy transfer along a food chain. The Sun may send us a large amount of energy but it is easy to see why it soon runs out. The transfer of energy at each level is very inefficient, usually between 2 and 5 %. So the number of steps in a food chain is always limited because there is no energy left. There are usually three steps in a chain, and rarely more than five. Fig 3 shows one way of illustrating the different ways in which energy is lost.

Fig 2
The energy transfer for an Antarctic food chain showing the percentage energy transfer at each level. At each stage over 90% of the available energy is lost as heat.

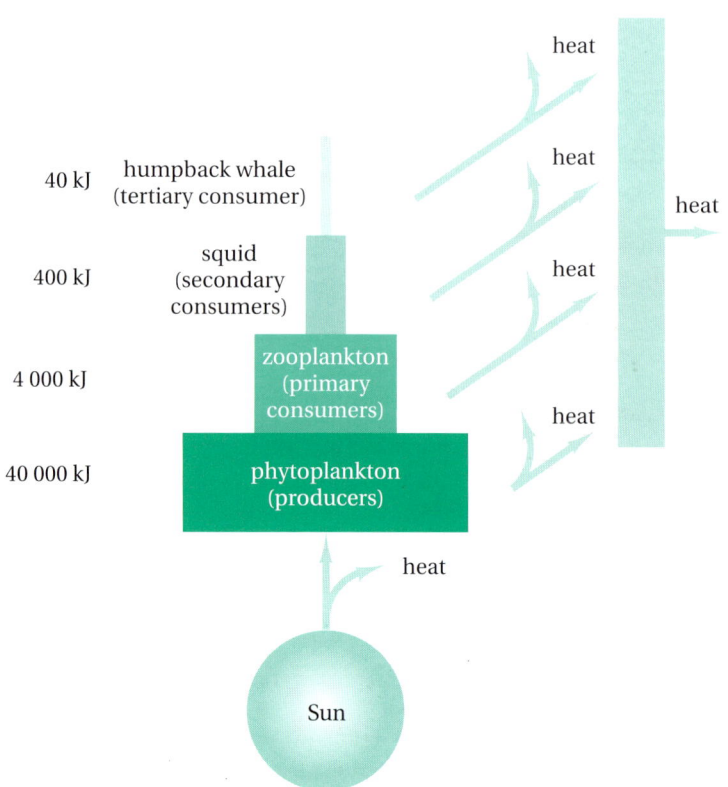

Fig 3
Energy transfer boxes for 4 different animals.

T = the total energy in the food eaten. Note that food that cannot be digested cannot be absorbed, so is not available to the organism
A = the energy that is absorbed
F = the energy that is lost in faeces
R = the energy lost in respiration
P = the energy incorporated into the tissues of the organism, this is the energy passed on to the next trophic level. An important trend here is that mammals pass a smaller proportion of their energy intake up the food chain because they use more energy to maintain temperature.

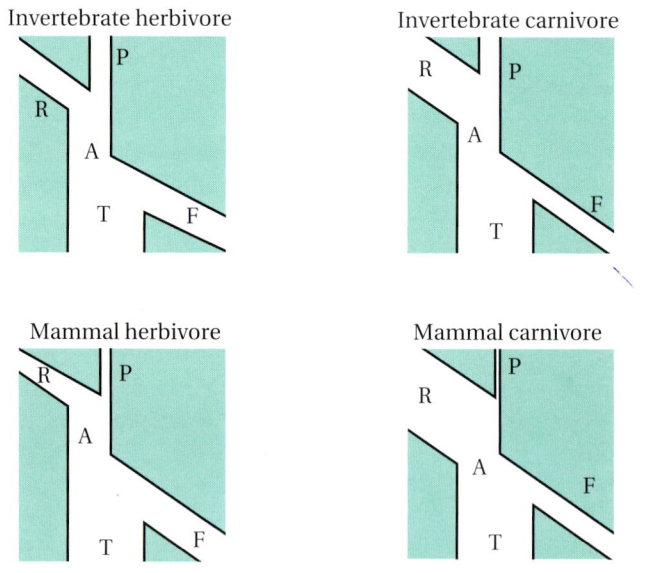

Ecological pyramids
Pyramid diagrams show the relative size of different components at each of the trophic levels. Three types of pyramid diagram are commonly used; **numbers**, **biomass** and **energy**.

1 Pyramids of numbers

These refer to the numbers of organisms in the different species in a food chain. Fig 4 shows examples of the main types of pyramids of numbers. Sometimes these are true pyramids – wide at the bottom and getting narrower towards the top. Other examples have a narrow base, followed by the usual pyramid shape. This happens when the producers are large e.g. trees. Pyramids can be inverted when parasites are involved. For the following food chain, the numbers of organisms may increase at each level:

oak tree → grey squirrel → flea

Food chain	Pyramid of numbers	Pyramid of biomass	Pyramid of energy
Fox Rabbit Grass			
Fleas Grey Squirrels Oak tree			
Shark Herring Zooplankton Phytoplankton			

> **E**
> When you see an inverted pyramid of numbers, where there are more secondary consumers than primary, think 'parasites' as an explanation.

> **E**
> Make sure you are clear about how energy is lost. During respiration a lot of energy is lost as heat because reactions are inefficient and only some of the energy is used to make ATP. When ATP is used – e.g. in muscular contraction, all of the remaining energy is eventually lost as heat.
>
> Common exam mistakes include statements like "energy is used for respiration" and some candidates even confuse respiration with photosynthesis.

Fig 4
The three types of pyramids for four different food chains

2 Pyramids of biomass

Biomass refers to the dry mass of the population within the ecosystem, and so takes into account the different size of organisms. There may be millions of aphids on an oak tree, but the mass of the tree far outweighs the mass of the insects feeding on it. Pyramids of biomass give a more realistic picture of feeding relationships, but they are very difficult or impossible to work out in practice because biomass refers to dry mass, which you cannot work out without killing the organism. So if you want to work out a pyramid of biomass for an African plain, you have to estimate the dry mass of the grass, zebra, antelope, lions etc in the food chain.

Pyramids of biomass are usually true pyramids, but there is one classic situation in which the consumers can outweigh the producers; in some areas of the ocean the mass of the zooplankton (minute animals) can outweigh the phytoplankton (minute plants) on which they feed. This is because the producers have a short life cycle and reproduce as fast as they are eaten.

3 Pyramids of energy

If you calculate the total amount of energy that flows *through* each trophic level you will always get a true pyramid. Even with the phytoplankton food chain the amount of energy flowing through the producers will be greater than that flowing through the primary consumers.

14.2 Nutrient cycles

The nitrogen cycle

Nitrogen is an essential component of several vital compounds, notably proteins and nucleic acids (RNA and DNA). The nitrogen cycle is summarised below and in Figs 5 and 6.`

- Plants generally absorb nitrogen as nitrate (NO^-_3); a soluble ion that is usually produced by microbes acting on nitrogen-containing compounds.

- Plants combine nitrate with the carbohydrate made in photosynthesis to make amino acids and nucleotides, the building blocks of proteins and nucleic acids.

- Nitrogen is passed up the food chain as animals eat the plants.

- Finally, all nitrogen ends up in non-living organic material. This could be dead leaves, dead bodies, faeces or urine (which contains nitrogen in urea or uric acid).

- The nitrogen-rich dead matter is broken down by decomposers – bacteria and fungi. These organisms obtain their nutrients by extra-cellular digestion (secretion of enzymes and absorbing the soluble products, such as amino acids). This process is called **saprophytic decay** and the end products are ammonium compounds (NH_4^+ ions).

- The last stage of saprophytic decay – the production of ammonium compounds from amino acids or other compounds – is called **ammonification**.

- The ammonium ions are used by **nitrifying bacteria**. These organisms are examples of **chemoautotrophs**. They obtain their energy from oxidation reactions rather than from the Sun. In this case, the bacteria obtain their energy from the oxidation of the ammonium ions. This is called **nitrification**.

Nitrification

Nitrification is a two-stage process:

- The ammonium ions are oxidised into nitrite (NO_2^-) ions by bacteria of the genus *Nitrosomonas*;

- The nitrite is further oxidised into nitrate (NO_3^-) ions by bacteria of the genus *Nitrobacter*;

Finally, the soluble nitrate is absorbed by plants and the cycle repeats itself.

As well as the main cycle described above, you also need to know how nitrogen can be lost from the cycle to the atmosphere - **denitrification** - and how it can be re-gained from the atmosphere; **nitrogen fixation**.

E Be careful to distinguish between the element nitrogen contained in compounds such as nitrates and protein, and nitrogen in the atmosphere. When referring to atmospheric nitrogen, always write "nitrogen gas".

The basic steps in the nitrogen cycle

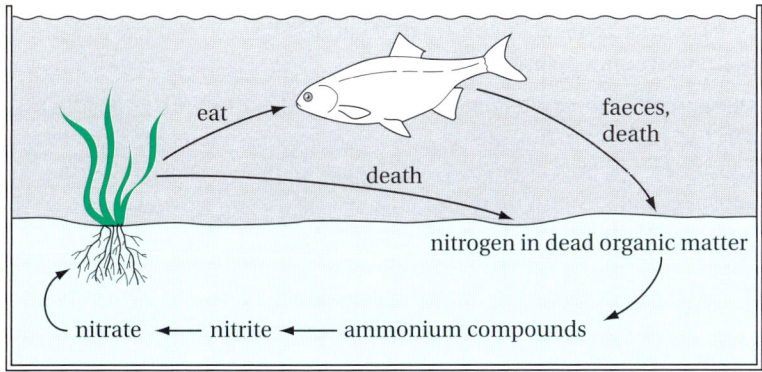

Fig 5
The nitrogen cycle in a fish tank

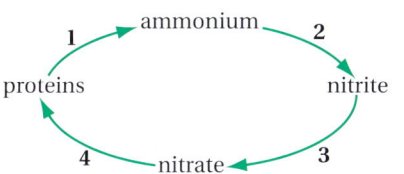

1 = saprophytic decay
2+3 = nitrification
4 = nitrogen passes up the food chain in organic molecules (mainly protein)

Fig 6
The nitrogen cycle in a nutshell

> **E**
> Learn the basic nitrogen cycle, as shown in Fig 6, before you attempt to learn all the complications.

Losing nitrogen from the atmosphere – denitrification

Denitrifying bacteria turn nitrate into nitrogen gas, thus enabling it to be lost from the nitrogen cycle. These bacteria are anaerobes and so thrive in waterlogged soil, stagnant water and other oxygen-starved areas.

Gaining from the atmosphere – nitrogen fixation

About 80% of the atmosphere is made up from nitrogen gas, but this is usually unavailable to living things. Molecules of N_2 gas have a triple ($N\equiv N$) bond that takes a lot of energy to break. When nitrogen gas is turned into soluble nitrogen ions, which are available to organisms, we say that nitrogen has been **fixed**. Nitrogen can be fixed during electrical storms, when the lightning provides enough energy to split the triple bond, so that the accompanying rain has dissolved nitrate in it. More reliably, however, bacteria can fix nitrogen. Nitrogen fixing bacteria, mainly of the genus **Rhizobium**, contain the enzyme **nitrogenase** that allows nitrogen gas to be fixed at low temperatures.

Nitrogen fixing bacteria can be free-living in water or soil, but they can also occur in the roots of some plants such as **legumes** (e.g. peas, beans and clover). These plants have a **mutualistic** relationship with Rhizobium; the plants get a supply of nitrate while the bacteria get some protection from predation and a supply of sugars. Legumes can thrive in nitrogen-poor soil, so growing a legume crop and allowing it to decay into the soil is a natural way to improve soil fertility.

NB The gene for the enzyme nitrogenase has now been isolated, which opens up the possibility that it can be inserted into the genome of other plants. In theory, these too will be able to fix their own nitrogen and reduce the need for fertiliser.

> **E**
> Make sure that you can distinguish between:
> 1 Nitrifying bacteria that turn ammonium into nitrates – 'the good guys';
> 2 Denitrifying bacteria that turn nitrates into nitrogen gas – 'the bad guys';
> 3 Nitrogen fixing bacteria that turn nitrogen gas into ammonia – 'the angels'.

There is very little carbon dioxide in the atmosphere; about 0.04 % – just 4 molecules in every ten thousand. The world's oceans, rivers and lakes contain more carbon dioxide dissolved in water as hydrogen carbonate (HCO_3^-) ions than occurs in gaseous form in the atmosphere. This explains why, on a global scale, most photosynthesis takes place in the oceans.

The carbon cycle

Carbon forms the backbone of all organic molecules that make up the bodies of organisms, including carbohydrates, lipids, proteins, nucleic acids and simpler organic molecules.

Overall, the carbon cycle involves carbon dioxide from the atmosphere – or hydrogen carbonate ions (HCO_3^-) in water – being fixed into organic molecules by photosynthesis, and then being released back into the atmosphere by respiration of the various organisms in the ecosystem. This gives us the very simple diagram shown in Fig 7.

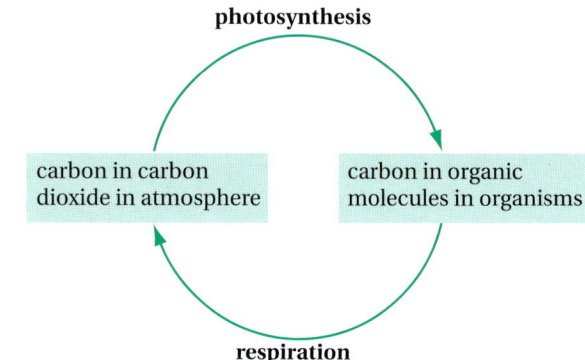

Fig 7
The two basic steps in the carbon cycle

Fig 8
A more detailed carbon cycle

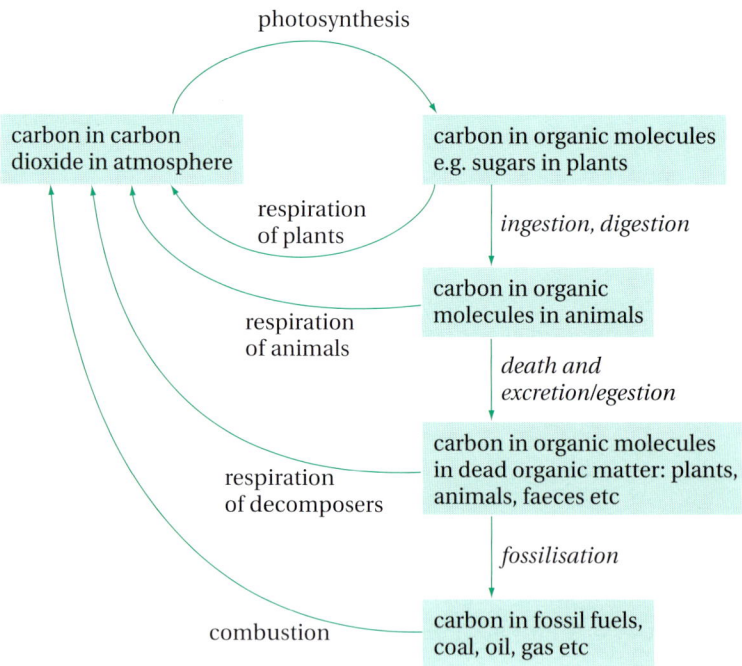

We can build on this simple cycle to show how carbon is passed up the food chain and is released back into the atmosphere by the respiration of the various organisms in the ecosystem (Fig 8). The carbon that is not released by respiration is trapped in fossil fuels such as coal, gas and oil and other deposits, such as peat. The only way this fossilised carbon can be released back into circulation is by **combustion**, which is increasing globally year on year. As we also reduce the global rate of photosynthesis by deforestation we are shifting the balance and increasing the amount of carbon dioxide – a greenhouse gas – in the atmosphere.

Photosynthesis is the only natural process that removes carbon dioxide from the atmosphere. Only carbon that is used to make structural compounds, such as cellulose, remains fixed. Thus global warming can only be reduced if more forests are planted and more carbon is fixed in young trees.

14.3 Studying ecosystems

Ecological techniques

Ecosystems are unbelievably complex, and to even begin to understand what is going on we must take careful measurements of both the organisms in an ecosystem and of the physical conditions that form their habitat. In this section, we look at some methods for sampling organisms and some techniques used to measure abiotic factors (physical features of the ecosystem).

D

- **Abiotic factors** *are the non-living factors that affect an organism. These include light intensity, temperature, wind movement, pH, humidity and many others. Table 2 shows some of the ways in which these factors can be measured.*

- **Biotic factors** *are the living factors that an organism, e.g. food supply, predation, competition (from other species and from individuals of the same species), disease.*

- **Density-dependent factors** *are factors that change with the size of the population. Food supply, for example, is usually density dependent – the larger the population, the greater the competition for food.*

Table 2
Measuring some abiotic factors

Factor organisms	Measured by	Effect of abiotic factor on organisms
Temperature	Thermometer/ thermal probe	Enzymes and therefore metabolism are very temperature sensitive. Metabolic systems only work efficiently within relatively narrow temperature ranges. If the temperature is too low, metabolism slows; if it is too high, enzymes can be denatured.
Humidity	Hygrometer – a hand held device	Affects the rate of evaporation; the higher the humidity, the lower the rate of evaporation. The effect of humidity determines the effectiveness of transpiration in plants and thermoregulation (sweating/panting) in animals.
Light intensity	Light meter or light sensor	Often a limiting factor in photosynthesis – which affects productivity of the whole ecosystem.
pH	pH meter or chemical (indicator) test	Enzymes are very pH sensitive – metabolism can be disrupted if conditions become too acid or alkaline.

Factor organisms	Measured by	Effect of abiotic factor on
Oxygen concentration in water	Oxygen-sensitive electrode or chemical test	Oxygen solubility in water is low and varies with temperature; the lower the temperature, the more oxygen will dissolve in it.
Carbon dioxide concentration	Gas analysis	Essential for photosynthesis – can be a limiting factor in some circumstances.
Wind speed	Anemometer (hand held device)	Affects both rate of evaporation and cooling, so has an impact on transpiration in plants and thermoregulation in animals.

Sampling techniques

Frame quadrats are sample areas of ground that are small enough to be studied in a short time. A square frame 50 cm by 50 cm is often used because the grid is manageable and portable (see Fig 9a). Quadrats are normally used to *compare one area of ground with another.* For example, you might want to compare the vegetation on a north and south facing side of a hill, or to compare the species diversity on mown and un-mown patches of ground. You obviously cannot count all the plants in the area, so you must sample, and you would usually do this by placing random quadrats. Methods of ensuring that the quadrats are random – i.e. without human bias – include mapping out the area into a grid pattern and selecting squares using random numbers from tables or from a computer program designed for this purpose.

Line transects are used to sample organisms along a line on order *to show a change from one area to another,* such as down a rocky shoreline or along sand dunes – see Fig 9b.

You should be able to explain the effects of factors such as temperature and pH in terms of kinetic energy of molecules and their effects in the tertiary structure of enzymes. This is a common topic for synoptic questions.

In exam answers, *throwing* quadrats is not a satisfactory way of placing quadrats randomly (even if that's what you did on your field trip).

Fig 9
Quadrats and transects
a Quadrats are usually used to sample different areas of ground. The area can be divided using a grid and quadrats are then placed in squares chosen at random. The experimenter may measure the occurrence of different species, and/or the percentage cover of the different species.

15

Fig 9
Quadrats and transects

b Transects are lines that allow us to sample along a changing habitat. Different types of transect include the belt transect, where quadrats are placed at intervals along the line, or point transects where the species touching a particular point on the line are recorded.

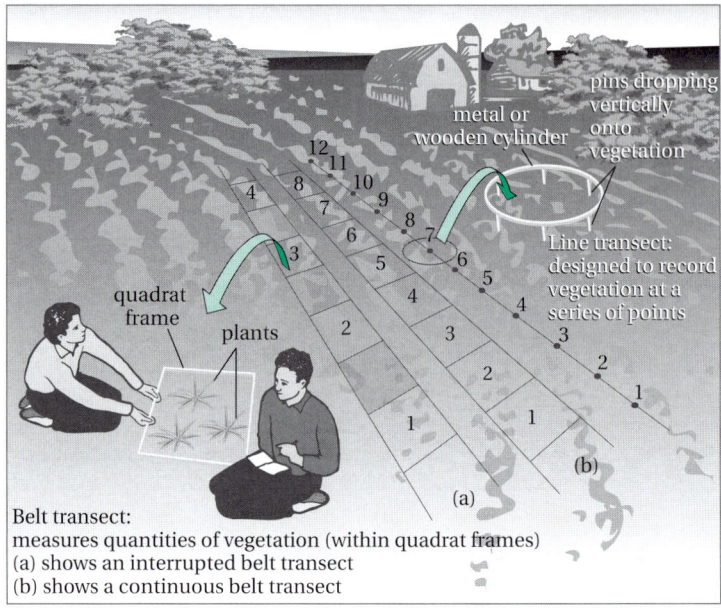

Belt transect:
measures quantities of vegetation (within quadrat frames)
(a) shows an interrupted belt transect
(b) shows a continuous belt transect

Standard deviation

Biological data almost always varies: height or blood pressure in humans, the number of fruit on a tree, the number of chicks raised in a year by a pair of thrushes etc. When such data is plotted on a graph a bell-shaped curve called a **normal distribution** is obtained (Fig 10). **Standard deviation** refers to *measure of the spread of such data about the mean.*

Fig 10

a Different normal distribution curves. The standard deviation in graph (i) is much greater than in graph (ii)

   (i) a narrow distribution curve

   (ii) a wide distribution curve

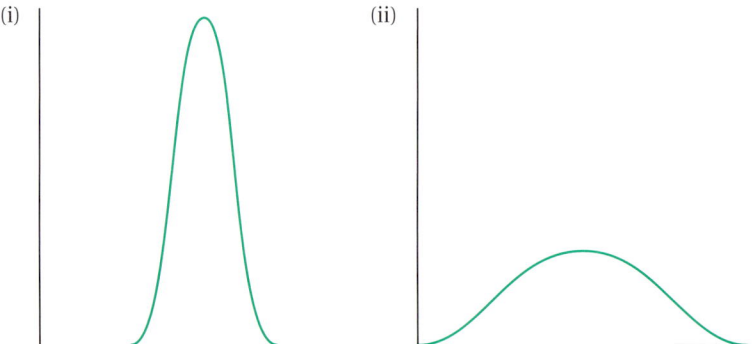

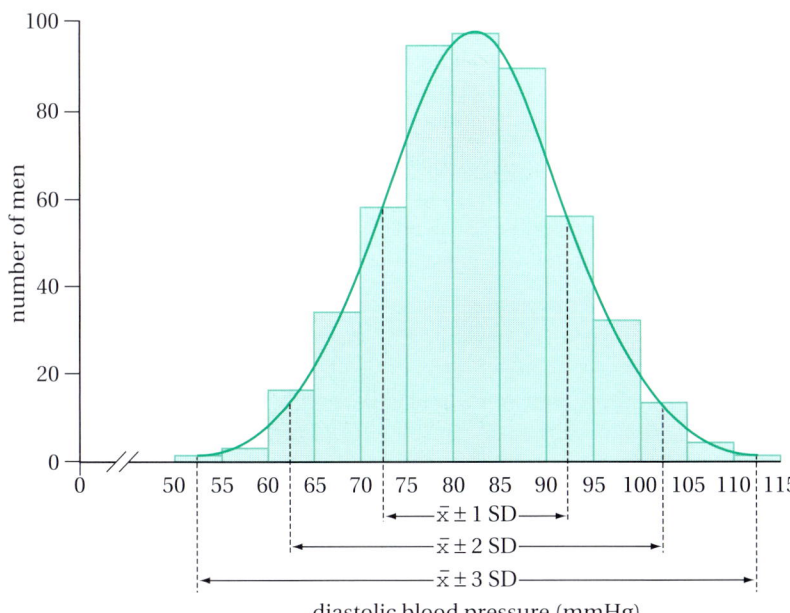

diastolic blood pressure (mmHg)

Fig 10
b The normal distribution of blood pressure. Note the key points of a normal distribution; values above and below the mean are equally common, small deviations from the mean are much rarer than large ones

Standard deviation is expressed in the same units as the original data. 68% of all measurements fall within one standard deviation either side of the mean, and 95% will fall within two standard deviations. From Fig 10b, the mean diastolic blood pressure is 82 mmHg and the standard deviation is 10 mmHg. So 68% of the readings fall between 72 and 92 mmHg, and 95% fall between 62 and 102 mmHg.

The formula for working our the standard deviation is

$$s = \sqrt{\frac{\Sigma(x - \bar{x})^2}{n - 1}}$$

Where s = the standard deviation,

Σ = the sum of

x = each measurement

$\bar{x}$ = mean measurement

n = the number of measurements

The null hypothesis and experimental design

In science, progress is made by a process of **conjecture** and **refutation**, which in plain English means thinking up an explanation for an observation; 'could this possibly be?', then gathering data, analysing it and coming to the conclusion 'no, it couldn't' or 'possibly, it could'. A vital point here is that you can never prove anything, but you can devise a hypothesis, test it and fail to disprove it, so you gather support for a particular idea.

> **E**
> Make sure that you understand when to use standard deviation and chi-squared tests, and what the results tell you. A common mistake is to state 'they tell you that your results are accurate'.

A hypothesis is a testable idea. There are two types:

1 The **experimental hypothesis** states that there will be a significant connection between cause and effect. An example could be 'alcohol slows down an individuals ability to do mental arithmetic'.

2 The **null hypothesis** takes the opposite standpoint, such as 'alcohol has no effect on an individual's ability to do mental arithmetic'. A key point here is that **statistical tests only test the null hypothesis**. Statistical tests are needed to tell you whether your results are due to chance or not

Chi squared is one statistical test that is used to decide whether results are **significant** or simply due to chance. Basically, the observed results are compared with those that you would expect of they were due to chance. The chi-squared test gives you a result in terms of probability. By convention, if the probability that your results are due to chance is **less than 5%** (or 0.05 as a decimal), you can say that they are significant and so reject the null hypothesis.

The Chi squared test; a case study

A group of scientists carried out an investigation into the preferred resting places of leopards in a game park in Tanzania, to see if there was a difference between males and females. They tracked two hundred leopards by sight, by radio collar and by analysis of their droppings. Their finding are shown in Table 3.

The null hypothesis for this investigation is 'There is no difference in the distribution of male and female leopards at rest'.

Table 3
The distribution of leopards

	In trees	In rocks	In open grassland	Row Total
Males	a 19	b 56	c 25	100
Females	d 51	e 26	f 23	100
Column Total	70	82	48	200 (grand total)

The formula for the chi-squared test is

$$\chi^2 = \Sigma \frac{(O - E)^2}{E}$$

Where Σ = the sum of all, O = observed and E = expected.

Having got our observed results from the field studies, how do we work out the expected results? For each category of box, we can work out the expected value E from the formula:

$$E = \frac{\text{Row total} \times \text{column total}}{\text{Grand total}}$$

For each box…

$$\text{Box a} = \frac{100 \times 70}{200} = 35$$

$$\text{Box b} = \frac{100 \times 82}{200} = 41$$

$$\text{Box c} = \frac{100 \times 48}{200} = 24$$

$$\text{Box d} = \frac{100 \times 70}{200} = 35$$

$$\text{Box e} = \frac{100 \times 82}{200} = 41$$

$$\text{Box f} = \frac{100 \times 48}{200} = 24$$

Having both the expected and observed values, one of the easiest ways to work out the value is chi-squared is to fill in a table like Table 4.

Box	Observed	Expected	O – E	$(O - E)^2$	$\dfrac{(O - E)^2}{E}$
a	19	35	−16	256	7.3
b	56	41	15	225	5.5
c	25	24	1	1	0.04
d	51	35	16	256	7.3
e	26	41	−15	225	5.5
f	23	24	−1	1	0.04

Fig 4
Working out the value of chi squared

Total = 25.68

The next step is to work out the degrees of freedom (D of F). This is a measure of the spread of the data; the more categories, the more degrees of freedom. The formula is

D of F = (no of rows −1) × (no of columns − 1) which in this case is
= (2 − 1) × (3 − 1) = 1 × 2 = 2

So we have a value of 25.68 with 2 degrees of freedom.

What next? To get a probability value (the whole point of the test) we look up these values in a table of chi-squared values.

Table 5
Chi squared values

Degrees of freedom	Probability					
	0.50	0.25	0.10	0.05	0.02	0.01
1	0.45	1.32	2.71	3.84	5.41	6.64
2	1.39	2.77	4.61	5.99	7.82	9.21
3	2.37	4.11	6.25	7.82	9.84	11.34
4	3.36	5.39	7.78	9.49	11.67	13.28

Table 5 shows that, with two degrees of freedom, the chances of obtaining a chi-squared value of 25.68 is less than 1%. This means there is a less than 1% probability that our results are due to chance (we only needed a value of 9.2 for 1% probability and 5.99 for the vital threshold of 5% probability). Values as high as 25 are only found when there is a marked difference in the observed and expected frequencies. From this was can reject the null hypothesis and accept the experimental hypothesis i.e. there is a difference in the habitats preferred by male and female leopards. Note that we have *gained support* for our theory, but we can *never prove* it to be correct.

Chi squared in examinations

You will not be asked to work through any examples of chi squared in examinations- it's far too time consuming and the examiners want to test your biology, not your maths. However, you may be expected to know the basic principles and uses of chi-squared so you may get questions like Q3 in the sample paper (see pages 33–34).

14.4 The dynamics of ecosystems

- **Ecosystem** – *a natural unit consisting of producers, consumers and decomposers together with non-living components. The conditions within a particular ecosystem are usually fairly uniform e.g. a pond, lake, coral reef or rainforest.*

- **Community** – *all of the organisms of all species in the ecosystem. The communities found in a particular habitat are based on dynamic feeding relationships, meaning that the size of a population is determined by other populations that it preys on, or that preys on it.*

- **Population** – *a group of individuals of the same species. The range of the population varies according to the species; the water fleas in a pond constitutes a population, but so does the entire human population on the planet.*

- **Habitat** – *where an organism lives. For small organisms the immediate surroundings – the **microhabitat** – is often of vital importance. For instance, aphids (e.g. greenfly) can usually by found on the underside of a leaf, next to a vein. If the individual moved a millimetre away the conditions would change – there would be less food available, and it may be more exposed to wind movements.*

- **Niche** – *a concept that explains an organism's place in the ecosystem. A niche is largely defined by what an organism eats (unless it's a plant), what eats it and what conditions it lives in. The **competitive exclusion principle** states that no two species can occupy precisely the same niche, so they don't compete for precisely the same resources.*

Stability of populations

Suppose you introduce a pair of rabbits onto an island. How would the population grow? Assuming that they were a healthy pair, and they managed to reproduce, the population growth would be something like that shown in Fig 11. This classic pattern is seen in many different situations; rats in a sewer, beetles in a sack of flour, elephants in a game reserve, even bacteria in your socks; only the timescale changes.

Fig 11
A generalised population
growth curve

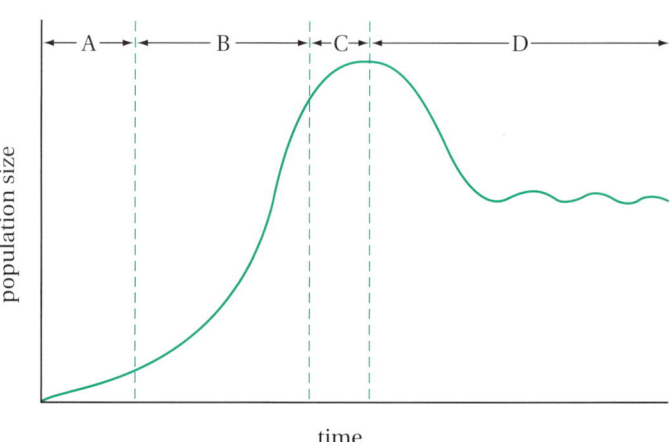

population size

time

The stages in the growth curve are:

1 **Lag phase** – a time of slow growth. There are many different reasons for the lag; one is that microorganisms may have to synthesise the enzymes needed to utilise a new food source. Species that reproduce sexually may take a while to grow and reach sexual maturity.

2 **Log (Logarithmic) or exponential phase** – a period of rapid and unrestricted growth. Conditions are favourable, plenty of food. The key point is; *no limiting factors.*

3 Growth slows due limiting factors. No population can go on increasing indefinitely, sooner or later there will be **environmental resistance** of some sort. Food may become scarce, waste may accumulate etc.

4 The population stabilises at its **carrying capacity**; the size of population that can be supported in a given area e.g. a pond may be able to support a population of 40 sticklebacks, but not more.

Factors affecting populations

No population can go on expanding indefinitely. The human population has been rising for thousands of years but even we cannot go on in the same way. If we carried on reproducing to our fullest capacity, a point will be rapidly reached when there is not enough food, too much overcrowding and disease. At the moment there are different rates of population growth in different parts of the world for various social and economic reasons.

Most populations are limited by a simpler set of factors than those that affect humans:

Competition All organisms are locked into a struggle to eat and not be eaten until they have a chance to reproduce. More organisms are born than can possibly survive and an inevitable consequence of this is **competition**. Common examples of competition include plants competing for light, soil water and minerals from the soil, while animals may compete for food, mates or nesting sites.

There are two types of competition:

Interspecific competition – competition between species. Badgers and foxes, for example, may compete for some of the same food sources and burrows. Some plants secrete chemicals that inhibit the growth of competing species.

Intraspecific competition – competition between individuals of the same species.

The development of an ecosystem

Before deforestation in the last thousand years or so, the UK was largely covered with **deciduous forest**. The dominant species were oak, ash, beech, birch and a couple of others. This is the **climax community** that develops in our temperate climate. Bears, lynxes and wolves roamed the countryside, the human population was small and their influence was negligible. Now there is very little 'natural' forest left – virtually none in England – and the forests that do exist were planted by humans.

So how did the forest develop in the first place? Ecosystems develop by the processes of **colonisation** and **succession** until the climax community is established (Fig 12).

> To remember which type of competition is which, **interspecific** competition is **between** species like **international** football matches are **between** nations.

> In questions about limiting factors, think carefully about the species involved. Organisms seldom run out of space – food and water supplies tend to run out long before organisms are standing shoulder to shoulder.

> In exam questions, avoid giving organisms human emotions. Trees do not *like* light, Woodlice are not '*happy*' in rotting vegetation and plants don't '*know*' when it's time to flower.

Deciduous (or broadleaf) trees lose their leaves in winter. In contrast some trees are evergreen e.g. the pine trees that dominate the forests of colder latitudes.

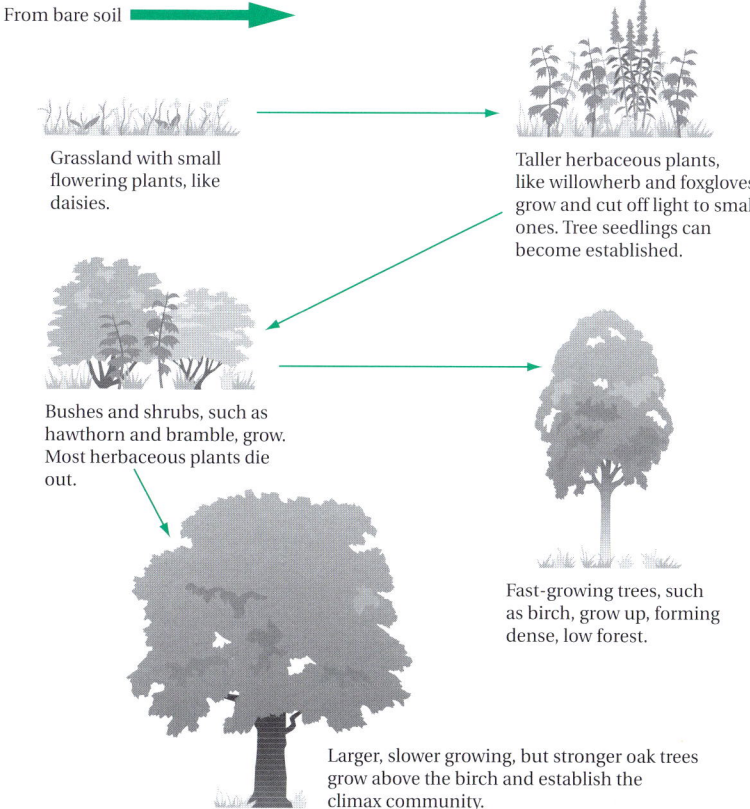

From bare soil

Grassland with small flowering plants, like daisies.

Taller herbaceous plants, like willowherb and foxgloves, grow and cut off light to small ones. Tree seedlings can become established.

Bushes and shrubs, such as hawthorn and bramble, grow. Most herbaceous plants die out.

Fast-growing trees, such as birch, grow up, forming dense, low forest.

Larger, slower growing, but stronger oak trees grow above the birch and establish the climax community.

Fig 12
Succession that occurs on a patch of bare ground, assuming little or no grazing.

The process of succession normally takes decades or centuries, but there are two common ways of studying the process:

1 Clear a patch of ground and watch what happens to the bare soil.

2 Study a sand dune system near a beach and observe the changes that occur as you move inland.

1 Clearing a patch of ground

Remove all the plants, fence it off from grazing animals, and observe the changes. The problem is that it takes at least fifty years, but eventually the forest is re-established. There are two conditions that need to be met of the ecosystem is to develop as normal;

- The soil must initially have relatively low humus content;

- There must be no grazing animals that can get onto the plot.

The main stages that you would observe as the ecosystem develops are:

- **Colonisation:** the bare soil is colonised by what we might think of as weeds - herbaceous plants that can grow in relatively nutrient-poor soil. They have a rapid life cycle, then die back and increase the humus content of the soil. Typical coloniser species are grasses, daisies, dandelions and clover.

- **Succession:** this occurs because the colonisers change the habitat. Once the colonisers have improved the quality of the soil, more species can grow. The **diversity** of herbaceous plants increases greatly as conditions become more favourable. Taller plants cut off the light and so out-compete the shorter ones. The greater diversity of plants attracts more insects that in turn attract birds and small mammals. At this stage grazing can have a marked effect and prevent any further succession. Many plants, including tree saplings, have their growing points at the top of the stem, and herbivores such as rabbits and sheep prevent any further growth. In contrast grasses grow from the base of the stem, so they thrive despite constant grazing.

- **Establishment of the climax community:** in the next phase small woody plants – shrubs such as hawthorn and bramble – begin to dominate. In turn these are out-competed for light by fast growing tree species like birch that form a low, dense forest. Eventually the large but slow growing trees – notably the oak - begin to dominate until the climax community is established and there is *no further succession.*

The climax community that develops depends on the climate. The process outlined above will not happen, for example, on exposed hillsides where the soil it too thin or the wind too harsh. Other examples of climax vegetation around the world include rainforest, cloud forest, tundra, grassland and coniferous forest.

2 Studying a sand dune system

Sand dunes are useful areas to study because you can observe colonisation and succession without having to wait 50 years. You can see some of the changes associated with the development of ecosystems as you simply walk inland (Fig 13). Near the sea the dunes are at their youngest – wind

---

Herbaceous plants have no woody tissue, in contrast to shrubs and trees.

E It is a good idea to learn one example of succession in detail, and make sure that you can name some plant *species* at each stage, rather then talking vaguely about 'trees and shrubs' etc.

tends to pile up the sand and the profile changes from year to year. Sand is a very difficult medium for plants; water and nutrients drain straight through, and the constant shifting makes it very difficult for the roots to anchor the plant. However some pioneer species, notably marram grass, has a dense root system that binds the sand together. This holds water and humus particles and makes the whole dune more permanent. Once the marram grass has made the environment less hostile, other plants such as ragwort, willow and grasses can take over. As you move inland the sand gets darker because the humus content increases – so does the species diversity.

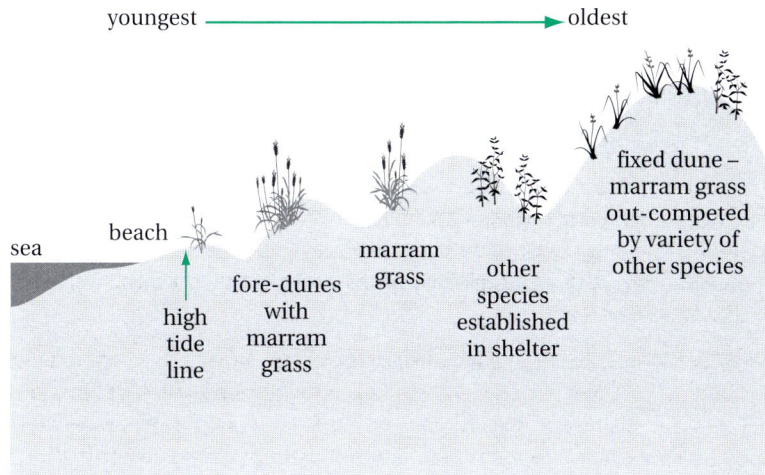

Fig 13
Sand dune succession

Succession from bare rock
Although our planet seems pretty crowded, there are still a few places where ecosystems can develop from scratch. A good example is the areas created by volcanic lava. As the lava cools it creates a barren hostile environment but even this can be colonised by organisms such as bacteria, fungi, algae and lichens. (You can often observe the same process beginning on the tiles on your roof).

As the rock weathers, soil particles gather in cracks so that mosses and other small, shallow-rooted plants can get a hold. As these plants spread they create yet more soil, which increases in both depth and nutrient content. Succession then takes place in the manner described above.

Species diversity
The numbers of different species that form the community of an ecosystem can vary greatly. Environments such as a coral reef or a rainforest show a **high species diversity** because conditions are generally favourable and stable. In these situations biotic factors – those due to other organisms – dominate organisms' lives. In contrast, in harsh environments such as the arctic or desert regions, there is **low species diversity** and abiotic factors such as temperature and water availability, dominate.

Lichens consist of algae growing inside a fungus. The fungus provides anchorage and protection from drying out. In turn the algae can photosynthesise and give the fungus organic compounds that would otherwise be unavailable from the bare rock.

14.5 Human influences on the environment

Ecological impact of farming

1 Monoculture

Until relatively recently, farms were diverse businesses where the farmers would grow several different crops, keep a variety of animals and perhaps have an orchard or two. The produce would be sold in local markets. But in today's supermarket-dominated food industry farmers are encouraged to grow a single crop such as oilseed rape or wheat, so that the supermarkets have fewer growers to deal with. The word **monoculture** refers to the growing of the same crop in large areas, often year after year. A particular crop will rapidly deplete the soil of specific nutrients at particular depths, and often lead to the accumulation of pests. Without humus to bind it together, soil becomes more powdery and is likely to be eroded by wind and rain, leading to dust storms and the accumulation of silt in rivers, lakes and oceans.

2 Removal of hedgerows

Hedgerows can be hundreds of years old, and represent an important habitat for many species. Farmers remove hedgerows for a variety of reasons:

- To enable them use large machinery more efficiently;

- To increase the area for growing crops;

- To avoid the need for maintenance (cutting etc);

- To prevent them shading the crops;

- To remove what is often seen as a reservoir of crop pests.

The loss of hedgerows has several disadvantages. Hedges, as well as being aesthetically desirable, shelter crops from wind and therefore minimise soil erosion. Without hedgerows, the species diversity of the countryside is lowered as many species of insect, plant, bird and small mammals lose their habitat.

3 Fertilisers

One of the key differences between agriculture and a natural ecosystem is that harvesting removes nutrients from the soil. Fertilisers are used to replace these nutrients. There are two types of fertilisers

- Organic – basically animal/human faeces/urine (sewage sludge or farmyard manure);

- Inorganic – liquid or (usually) pellets containing mineral ions, mainly nitrate, phosphate and potassium.

Both types are added to crops with the same basic aim; to increase crop yield. Both provide mineral ions, but with manure, the release of ions is gradual as the manure is decomposed by microbial action. The advantages and disadvantages are discussed in Table 6 below.

Type of fertiliser	Advantages	Disadvantages
Organic	• Cheap – farms often generate their own; • Not easily lost by leaching; • Improves soil - better humus levels, water retention, aeration and texture	• Variable (usually low) nutrient content; • Slow release of nutrients; difficult/ expensive to store and handle; • May contain plant or animal pathogens that cause disease; • May contain metal residues that are passed into food chain; • Requires heavy machinery that can compact soil
Inorganic	• Exact composition known – soil balance can be controlled; • Easy to store and handle; • Can be applied with light machinery – avoids soil compaction	• Expensive – it's a commercial product; • Most components soluble - rapid leaching into rivers; • Applied in concentrated form – can cause osmotic damage to plants; • Can cause acidification of soil

Table 6
 Organic v inorganic fertiliser

Problems with fertiliser

Traditionally, farmers used organic fertiliser (cow dung and the like) to maintain the fertility of the soil. Today, when many farms have no animals, this is increasingly difficult and farmers turn to inorganic fertilisers that can deliver exactly the right nutrients to the crop. This can cause problems because large amounts of the fertiliser can be washed away (leached) into rivers and lakes. This causes **eutrophication**, a nutrient build-up that results in the water being over-fertile. The process is summarised in Fig 14.

Fig 14
A summary of eutrophication

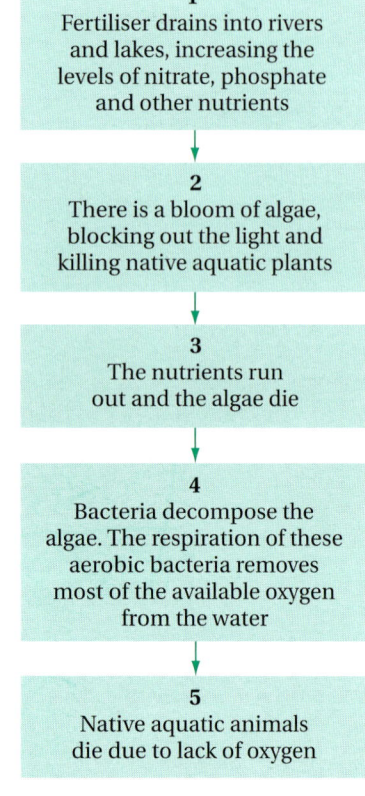

1
Fertiliser drains into rivers and lakes, increasing the levels of nitrate, phosphate and other nutrients

2
There is a bloom of algae, blocking out the light and killing native aquatic plants

3
The nutrients run out and the algae die

4
Bacteria decompose the algae. The respiration of these aerobic bacteria removes most of the available oxygen from the water

5
Native aquatic animals die due to lack of oxygen

E Note that the algae themselves do not reduce the oxygen content. They photosynthesise, so actually increase the oxygen levels for a short while

Biochemical oxygen demand (BOD)

This is a method of assessing the quality of a water sample by measuring bacterial activity. The more organic matter (e.g. sewage) in the water the more aerobic bacteria there will be, and the more oxygen they will use. A BOD test is performed as follows:

- Collect two water samples from the same site;

- Measure the oxygen content of one sample;

- Seal the other sample in an airtight container and incubate it in the dark at 20 °C for five days (if it were not dark the photosynthesis of algae would produce oxygen and interfere with the result);

- Measure the oxygen concentration of the second sample. The difference in the two readings is the BOD. The higher the BOD, the more contaminated the water sample.

Pesticide toxicity

Pesticides are widely used on our farmland. Examples include:

- Herbicides to kill weeds that compete with our plant crops;

- Insecticides to kill the insect pests such as aphids;

- Fungicides to kill common crop diseases like potato blight and mildew;

- Molluscicides to kill mollusc pests such as slugs and snails.

One of the first pesticides to be widely used was DDT in the 1950s and 60s. It became obvious that it was affecting food webs and its use was banned in 1972.

A major problem with pesticides like DDT is that of **bioaccumulation**. DDT is fat soluble, and most organisms can only excrete water-soluble chemicals. Thus DDT accumulates in the fatty tissues of organisms. Fig 15 illustrates the problem; if a pesticide gets into waterways it can be absorbed by the algae and - as it can't be excreted - will stay in the organism until it's eaten (or dies). Then, if a small animal eats, say 500 individual algae, it will accumulate all of their DDT. In this way the concentration is multiplied up the food chain, reaching a maximum in the apex (top) predator. The effect of the pesticide depends on the concentration, but symptoms in predatory birds such as herons include laying thin-shelled eggs or even result in the death of the adult birds.

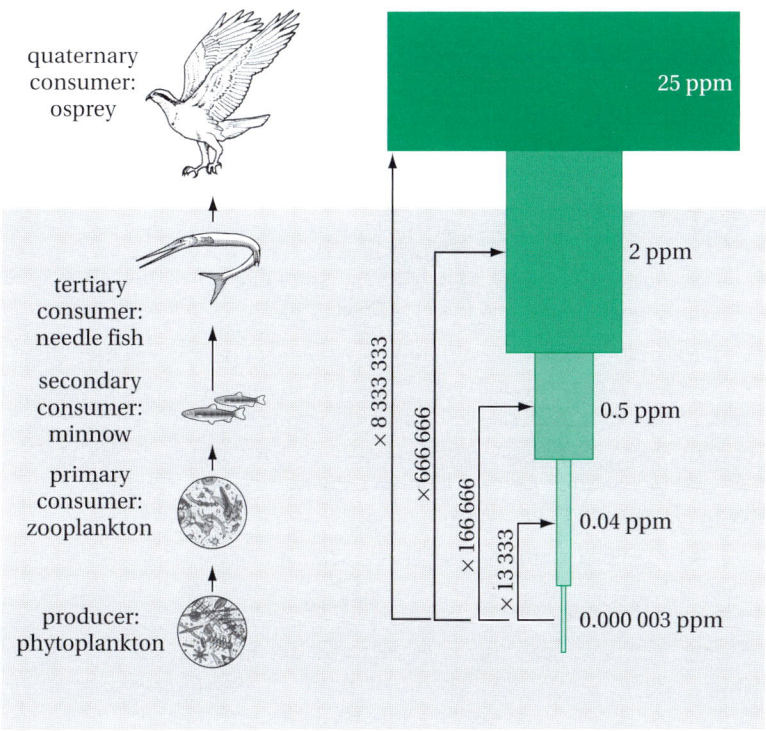

Fig 15
Bioaccumulation of DDT through an aquatic food chain

All licensed pesticides are tested to see that that they meet certain safety guidelines. The perfect pesticide is cheap, stable and easy to store. It should be safe to administer and will only affect the intended target. Having had its effect, it should **biodegrade** into harmless products due to the action of decomposers, and have no effect on the ecosystem. However, no pesticide meets all the criteria; one that is stable will tend to persist in the environment, for example. Ecosystems are complex and cannot be recreated in the lab, so it is almost impossible to predict the long-term effect of using these agrochemicals.

When an exam question asks you to evaluate, you need to give clear points on *each side* of the argument.

Biodegradable substances are broken down in the environment by the action of bacteria and/or fungi.

Balance of food production and conservation

For economic reasons, farmers are under great pressure to

- Concentrate on a small number of crops and grow these in large areas of monoculture;

- Remove hedgerows to make more growing space and to make the use of heavy machinery easier;

- Use large amounts of chemical fertilisers to increase yield from the depleted soil;

- Drain marshy areas and remove woodland;

- Use a wide variety of pesticides.

The two activities of producing food and conservation would seem to be exclusive, but they are not. There are several strategies that farmers can adopt to minimise damage to the environment:

- Use more organic manure, which improves soil structure by providing more humus so retaining more water. As the humus decays the nutrients are released slowly so there is less chance of them being leached away;

- Delay the application of chemical fertilisers until the main growing season so that more is absorbed before it is washed away;

- Leave crop stubble over the winter (i.e. plough later) so that there is less bare soil blow away;

- Rotate crops – growing a different crop year on year makes better use of minerals available at each soil depth. It also prevents the accumulation of crop-specific pests;

- Practice set aside – leave areas of wilderness to develop;

- Stop destroying hedgerows.

A2 5 Sample module test

Section A

1   The table below shows some figures relating to the flow of energy through a grassland ecosystem.

	Insect primary consumer	Mammal primary consumer	Insect secondary consumer	Mammal secondary consumer
Consumed as food	4.1	24.9	0.17	0.16
Absorbed from gut into body	1.6	12.5	0.14	0.13
Egested as faeces	2.5	12.4	0.03	0.03
Production of new tissue	0.64	0.25	0.05	0.01
Production of new tissue	0.96	12.25	0.09	0.12

a   Suggest units for the figures in the table

.... kj m⁻² per h .... *(1 mark)*

b   i   In primary consumers, what percentage of the energy absorbed from the gut into the body is lost in respiration in:

an insect

Answer = ...%

a mammal

Answer = ...% *(1 mark)*

ii   Suggest a reason for the difference in these figures between the two animals.

....

....

....

.... *(2 marks)*

c   Explain why the total energy consumed as food by the secondary consumers is less than the total energy consumed as food by the primary consumers.

less energy available as up to 90% lost each trophic level through faeces, respiration as heat

(2 marks)

Total 6 marks

2 A group of students was asked to investigate the factors affecting the distribution of plants in part of a woodland habitat. They decided to use a transect. The group first measured some of the abiotic factors along the transect. Their results are shown in the diagram below:

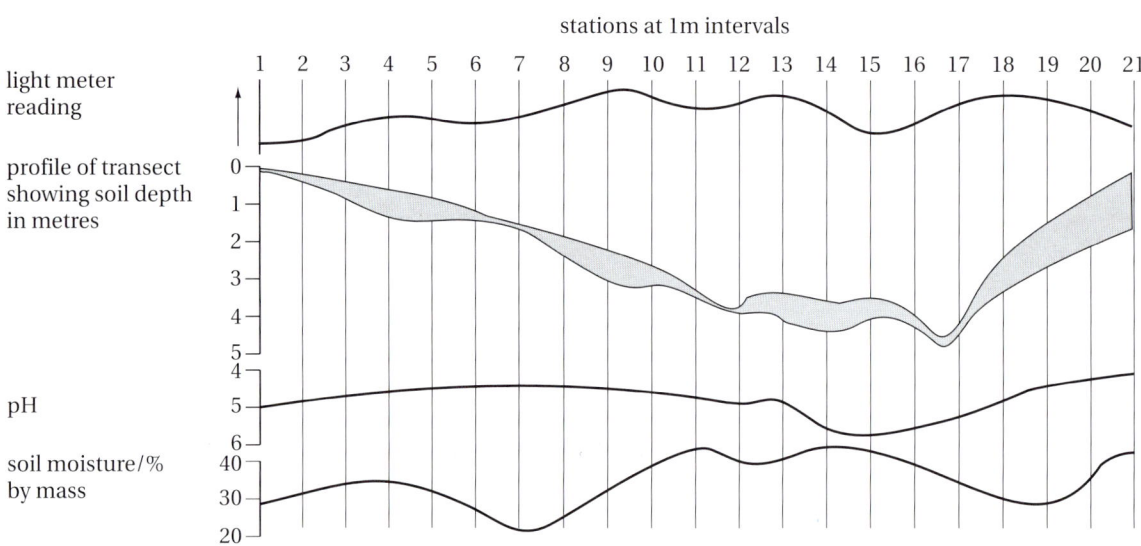

They then used a point quadrat to measure the distribution of plants along a transect. Below is an extract from the field notebook they used to record their results.

	Percentage hits at station																			
	1	2	3	4	5	6	7	8	9	10	11	12	13	14	15	16	17	18	19	20
Speedwell	20	5	15	5											5					
Dog's mercury		15		50	30	30			35	30										
Stinging nettle															60					
Bare ground		5	30	15		60	65	25		20	75	20		15		50	80	55	80	100

a   Describe how a point quadrat is used to measure the frequency of plants along a transect.

Evey time randomly choose points on transect put quadrat down and record what in it

(2 marks)

b   From these data, suggest and explain **one** reason for the distribution of speedwell along the transect.

light intensity. As present 1-4 with low " " also low L I at 15 + speedway present there

(2 marks)

Total 4 marks

3 Most cereal fields in Britain are sprayed with selective herbicides. In order to conserve wildlife, farmers are recommended to leave unsprayed a 6 metre strip, called a headland, around each cereal field.

a   Explain how spraying selective herbicides on a headland might affect the number of insects living there.

Insects die as might food on plants killed by herbicide. lead to competition or increased predation insects die as lack of food source

(2 marks)

b   The table below shows the results of an investigation to find the effect of leaving headlands unsprayed on the populations of butterflies living there.

Butterfly species	Number of each species recorded on headland sprayed with selective herbicide	Number of each species recorded on headland not sprayed with selective herbicide	x^2	Signficance (NS= not significant)
Small kipper	2	41	35.4	P<0.001
Large kipper	1	17	14.2	P<0.001
Large white	38	56	3.4	NS
Holly blue	13	29	6.1	P<0.05
Hedge brown	59	93	7.6	P<0.05
Small heath	0	11	11.0	P<0.01
Ringlet	23	52	11.2	P<0.01

i   Why was a χ^2 (chi-squared) test applied to the results?

To establish if relationship between sprayed areas + un sprayed

(1 mark)

ii   What conclusions can be drawn from the results of the chi-squared test?

direct correlation between sprayed and unsprayed. Butterflies do much better apart from luge white where no statistical evidence. But definitely affect kippers

(3 marks)

Total 6 marks

4 In organic farming, chemical weed-killers are not used on crops. Weeds have to be kept down manually. The number of weeks that can grow and the number of difference species vary with the type of crop. The drawings below show the weeds in barley and potato crops in two fields on an organic farm.

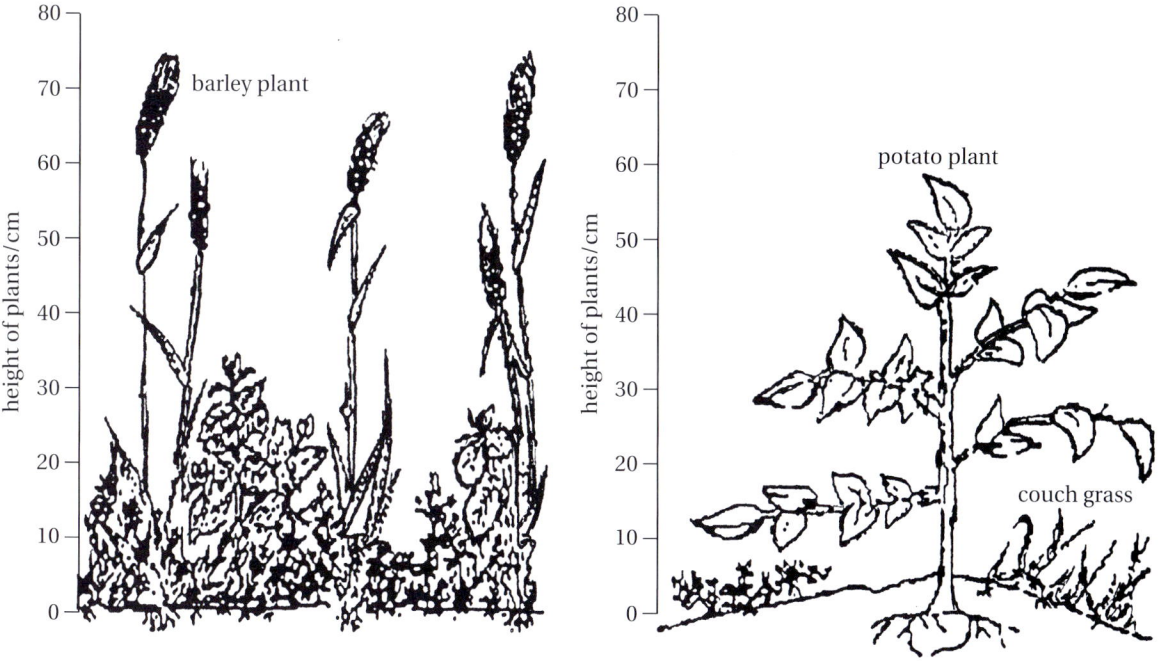

a   Use the information from the drawing to suggest one explanation for the fact that there are more weeds in the barley crop than in the potato crop.

couch grass out competed by larger area
taken up by width r size of potato
plant

.... *(2 marks)*

b One of the weeds in the barley fields is couch grass. In a laboratory investigation, scientists found that when couch grass and barley were germinated at the same time and the seedlings were grown close together during their development, the yield from the barley plants was the same as if they were grown alone. If couch grass was sown 14 days before barley, the yield from the barley plants was significantly smaller than when they were grown alone.

One hypothesis to explain these results is that older couch grass roots produce a substace that inhibits the growth of younger barley roots.

   i Briefly describe how this hypothesis might be tested.

   ....

   ....

   ....

   ....

   ....

   ....

   ....

   .... *(3 marks)*

   ii Suggest **one** alternative hypothesis to explain the results.

   ....

   ....

   ....

   .... *(1 mark)*

   Total 6 marks

5 The wren is a small, insect-eating bird. The percentage change is size of the wren population from one year to the next was estimated over a number of years. The number of days with snow lying in the previous winter was also recorded. This information is shown on the graph below:

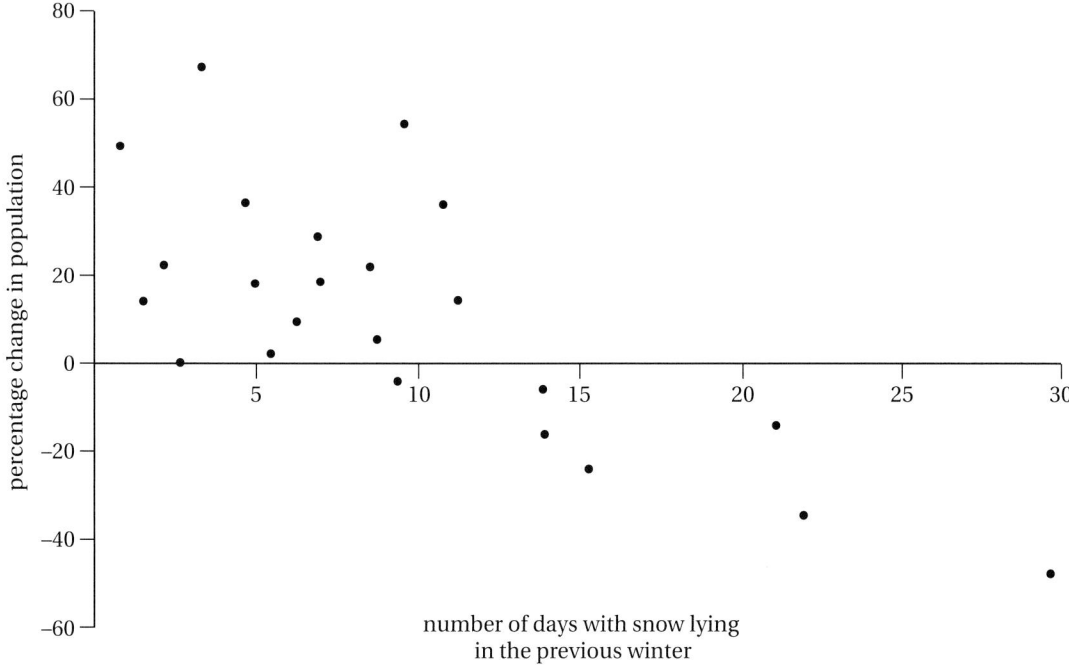

a   i   Describe the relationship between the number of days with snow lying and the change in population size.

....

....

....

.... *(2 marks)*

ii   Suggest and explain a reason for this relationship.

....

....

....

.... *(2 marks)* b   A comparison was made between the number of breeding pairs of wrens each year and their breeding success.

Number of breeding pairs of wrens/millions	Percentage increase in population size
5.9	55
1.9	48
5.10	35
5.11	25
5.12	2

Suggest an explanation for the relationship between the size of the breeding population and breeding success.

....

....

....

....   *(2 marks)*

Total 6 marks

6 Read the following passage.

Unlike most other mammals, bats do not have a steady body temperature. In flight, their body temperature of 42 °C and pulse rate of 1000 per minute are much higher than the 37 °C and 75 per minute of humans. At rest their temperature falls to the surrounding temperature, helping to conserve energy.

British bats feed mainly on insects caught in flight. During summer one pipistrelle bat may eat up to 3500 insects each night.

Bats put on about one third extra body mass during autumn and then hibernate from October to April. Their body temperature approximates to that of their surroundings, which may be as low as 0 °C.

Bats should never be disturbed during hibernation as, if they are, they may not survive the winter.

a   Suggest why British bats are unable to remain active during winter.

....

....

....

....   *(2 marks)* b   i   Use information from the extract to explain how British bats survive without feeding during winter.

....

....

....

....   *(2 marks)*

ii   Explain why bats may not survive the winter if frequently disturbed.

....

....

....

....   *(2 marks)*

Total 6 marks

7   The diagram below shows a section through a leaf. The plant from which it was taken was growing in normal conditions in an environment where water was readily available.

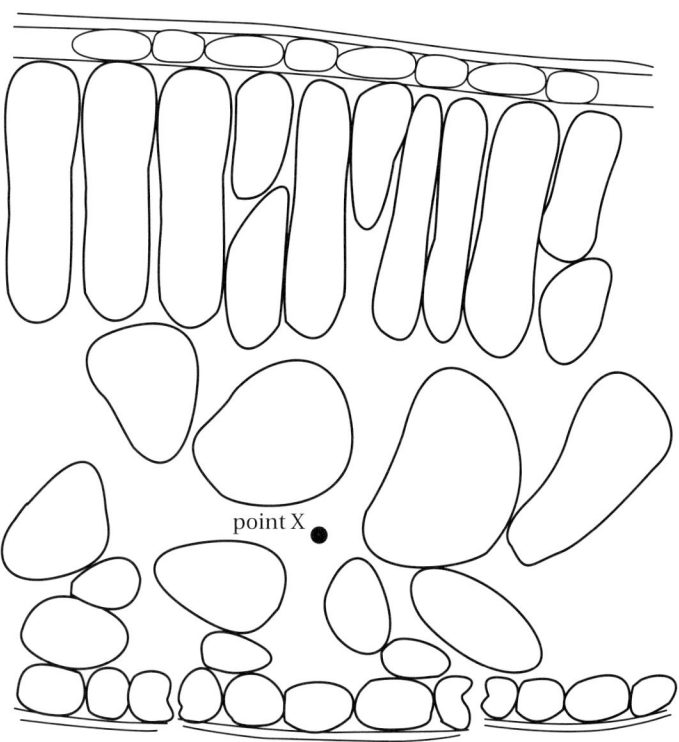

point X

a   Describe and explain how the oxygen concentration at Point **X** would vary over a 24-hour period.

....

....

....

....   *(2 marks)*

b   Explain, in terms of water potential, how

   i   Water is lost from a leaf during transpiration:

....

....

....

....

....

....

....

....   *(4 marks)*

   ii   The relative humidity of the atmosphere around the leaf may affect the rate of transpiration.

....

....

....

....   *(2 marks)*

Total 8 marks

Section B

8 An investigation was carried out into the microbial decomposition of leaf litter, using bags made out of netting with a fine mesh (0.3 mm^2). A large number of leaves were placed into these bags and buried in the leaf litter. The bags were then examined at monthly intervals.

a i The investigation showed that leaf decomposition occurred more rapidly during the months with higher average temperatures. Suggest **one** reason why this occurred.

....

.... *(1 mark)*

ii Suggest and explain how any **other** environmental factor could influence the rate of leaf decomposition.

....

....

....

.... *(2 marks)*

b Some of the carbon from carbon compounds in the leaf litter is eventually incorporated into carbon compounds in newly grown leaves. Suggest what living processes might be involved in this recycling of carbon and describe the contribution each makes to the recycling.

....

....

....

....

....

....

....

....

....

.... *(3 marks)*

Total 9 marks

9 A field was planted with grass and clover. After planting, half the field was used for cattle grazing and half was left ungrazed. Five years later a biologist collected samples of clover seeds from both parts of the field and grew them in an experimental plot. The diagram below shows clover plants grown from seeds gathered from grazed and ungrazed areas. Both sets of seeds were germinated and grown in identical conditions.

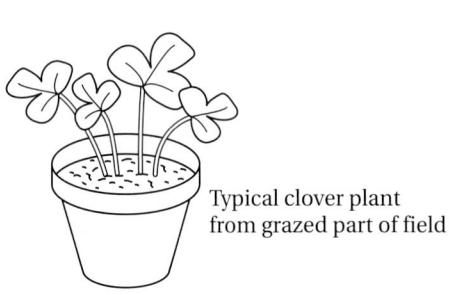

Typical clover plant from grazed part of field

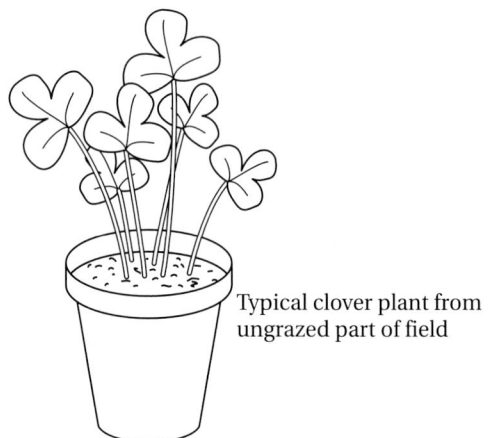

Typical clover plant from ungrazed part of field

a   The clover plants grown from the seeds gathered in the ungrazed part of the field were noticeably smaller than those grown from seeds collected in the grazed area. Suggest how this difference arose.

....

....

....

....

....

....

....

.... *(4 marks)*

b   It was suggested that, although these two kinds of clover differed in height, they were the same species. Describe how you would test this hypothesis.

....

....

....

....

....

....   *(3 marks)*

c   If the ungrazed portion of the field were left completely ungrazed for a much longer period than five years, what ecological changes would be observed, and why?

....

....

....

....

....

....

....

....

....

....

....   *(5 marks)*

Total 12 marks

Mark scheme for sample paper

Section A

1 a   Any unit of energy plus area plus time   *1*

   b   i   60% and 90%   *1*

   ii   Mammas need to maintain high body temperature; therefore need more energy/respire more   *2*

   c   Only a limited amount of energy is available; some lost at each stage of food chain; by respiration/as heat   *2*

(Max 6)

2 a   i   Place at right angles to tape at regular intervals (randomly = 0); record number of each type of plant touched by pin   *2*

   b   Only found at low light intensity; valid explanation eg. May not be able to compete at high light intensities/ may have high transpiration rate therefore cannot live in the open   *2*

(Max 4)

3 a   Reduced numbers because food plants of some insects killed by herbicide; these insects might be food source for other insects   *2*

   b   i   To accept or reject null hypothesis/to see if differences were significant   *1*

   ii   Spraying had no effect on population of large white; Spraying almost certainly affected population of skippers/less than 1 in 1000 possibility that reduction due to some other factor; Greater chance that reduction in population of other butterflies by chance/ less than 1 in 100 or five hundred.   *3*

(Max 6)

4 a   eg. Potato leaves have much larger surface area than barley leaves; weeds less able to compete for light   *2*

   b   Sow two sets of couch grass plants in pots, then 14 days later sow barley seeds in each pot; in one pot, separate the couch and barley roots by eg. plastic barrier; compare yields of mature barley plants, if plants in pots where roots were separated produce greater yield then hypothesis supported.   *3*

   c   eg. couch grass more effective competitor for mineral salts   *1*

(Max 6)

5 a   i   The more days of snow the lower the increase in population; above 12 days of snow decrease in population   *2*

   ii   Fewer birds to breed; explanation using data, eg. food hidden under snow   *2*

   b   More breeding pairs produces more competition; less breeding success   *2*

(Max 6)

6 a   eg. Few insects in winter; bats need large numbers to survive   *2*

   b   i   Extra body mass contains energy store needed to survive when not feeding; body temperature drops approaching 0 °C, conserving energy stores   *2*

   ii   Metabolic rate increased; energy stores used up   *2*

(Max 6)

7 a   Higher during the day because of photosynthesis; lower at night because of respiration   *2*

   b   i   Higher concentration of water molecules in leaf; water potential higher than outside air; water diffuses along water potential gradient; out via stomata   *4*

   ii   Smaller water potential gradient; since high relative humidity means higher concentration of water molecules; therefore lower rate of water loss from leaf   *max 2*

(Max 8)

Section B

8 a   i   eg Breakdown enzymic – enzyme activity higher at higher temperatures

                                                    1

        ii   eg. Soil content; water needed for hydrolysis   *2*

     b   Ingestion /absorption by microbes; microbial respiration; carbon compounds – carbon dioxide released into atmosphere:

absorbed by mature leaves; photosynthesis; in chloroplasts; sucrose; translocated to new leaves; via phloem   *6*

(Max 9)

9 a   Natural variation in height of plants; in ungrazed area, tall plants competed successfully with other plants for light; taller plants more likely to survive; and pass on genes to next generation; proportion of taller plants in population increases   *max 4*

     b   Interbeed the two types of clover; see if offspring produce; if offspring are fertile they are the same species   *3*

     c   Succession would occur; competition; arrival of new species; mechanism eg; airborne seeds; increased species diversity; modification of habitat eg, increased soil humus; development of shrubs; development of trees; plants that are not shade-tolerant may die out

                                    max 5

(Max 12)

Collins Support Materials for AQA – ORDER FORM

This booklet covers one module from the AQA Biology (A) course at A-level.
If you would like to order further copies from the series, please send a completed copy of this page to Collins by post or fax.

Title	ISBN	Price	Approval copy	Order quantity
1 Core Principles	000327709 7	£4.50		
2 Genes and Genetic Engineering	000327710 0	£4.50		
3 Physiology and Transport	000327711 9	£4.50		
4 Energy, Control and Continuity	000712416 3	£5.99		
5 Environment	000712417 1	£5.99		
TOTAL ORDER VALUE				

Details of other A-level titles in this series are available on our website:

www.**Collins**Education.com
Online support for schools and colleges

Also available: **Collins Advanced Modular Sciences – Biology**
comprehensive textbooks to support the new AQA (B) specification

Title	ISBN	Price	Approval copy	Order quantity
Biology AS	000327751 8	£18.99		
Biology A2	000327752 6	£17.99		
A2 Applied Ecology	000327741 0	£9.99		
A2 Microbes and Disease	000327742 9	£9.99		
A2 Behaviour & Populations	000327743 7	£9.99		
TOTAL ORDER VALUE				

Please fill in your details and send your order to the address below:

Name	Tel: 0870 0100 442
Address	Post: Collins Educational HarperCollins Publishers FREEPOST GW2446 GLASGOW G64 1BR
	Fax: 0141 306 3750
Post Code	Email: Education@harpercollins.co.uk